Table of Contents

STEP ONE: USING CONTEXT CLUES

continued on next page

-continued from previous page

STEP TWO: FUN WITH WORDS

STEP THREE: LANGUAGE TRICKS

STEP FOUR: READING SKILLS

©1983, Instructional Fair, Inc.

Things I Like to Do

Put the letter of the picture on the line where it fits.

_____ 1. I like to swim in the _____.

_____ 2. At school, it is fun to play on the

_____ .

_____ 3. At home, I like to watch _____.

_____ 4. Outside, we throw a _____.

_____ 5. Sometimes we build sand

_____ .

_____ 6. And making _____ is fun, too.

A.   B.   C.

D. 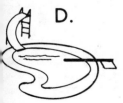   E.   F.

Begin Step 1   Using Context Clues

1

Which Picture?

Circle the picture that makes the best sense.

1. Airplanes fly high in the _____.

2. They go faster than a _____.

3. Some airplanes fly over the _____.

4. Many _____ can ride in one airplane.

5. You get _____ to eat on big planes.

2

Good Things to Eat

Put the letter of the picture on the line where it fits.

_____ 1. For fruit, I like apples and _____ .

_____ 2. For breakfast, I like a bowl of _____ .

_____ 3. And I love to drink _____ .

_____ 4. For supper, a chicken _____ is great.

_____ 5. But best of all is an _____ .

A.   B.

C.    D.   E.

3

Shipwreck!

Put the letter of the picture on the line where it fits. Be careful! There is one picture too many.

_____ 1. The big ship started to _____ .

_____ 2. The _____ got into a rowboat.

_____ 3. Soon they landed on a little _____ .

_____ 4. On their _____ , they asked for help.

_____ 5. Soon a _____ picked them up.

A.   B.   C.

D.    E.   F.

4

The Birthday Wish

Read each sentence. Use the given letter to help choose the right word. Write the word in the space.

1. I want a b_____ for my birthday.

   cake   bike   brown

2. I can ride a bike f_____.

   fast   fish   good

3. I will have bike r_____ with my friends.

   roads   fun   races

4. A new bike will cost a lot of m_____.

   money   morning   toys

5. I will let my s_____ ride it, too.

   mother   sister   surprise

5

Fire!

Read each sentence. Use the given letter to help choose the right word. Write the word in the space.

1. A fire t_____ came down the street.

   truck   train   man

2. The house across the s_____ was on fire.

   street   story   park

3. The firemen put w_____ on the fire.

   window   paper   water

4. A fireman ran into the h_____.

   house   school   hurry

5. He came out with a b_____ and a kitten.

   toy   baby   big

6

Playing Dolls

Read each sentence. Use the given letter to help choose the right word. Write the word in the space.

1. I like to play with my grandmother's old
   d_____.

   dark   doll   toys

2. It has on a long, full d_____.

   coat   dinner   dress

3. I am very c_____ not to break it.

   cover   happy   careful

4. My b_____ has a cowboy doll
   that he likes.

   brother   bunny   neighbor

5. We play like the dolls lived long
   a_____.

   about   ago   always

7

Cops and Robbers!

Read each sentence. Use the given letter to help choose the right word. Write the word in the space.

1. Two men ran out of the b_____.

   book   bank   circus

2. Both of them had g_____.

   guns   gray   money

3. A policeman began to c_____ them.

   clean   chase   shoot

4. He ran fast and c_____ them.

   close   stopped   caught

5. They had taken lots of d_____ from the bank.

   money   dishes   dollars

Here's A Clue

Circle the correct word that answers the clue.

1. Children sit on this.

   chin   chair   chop

2. It goes on water.

   boat   bat   bear

3. You can live in it.

   house   hill   horse

4. It is a pet.

   den   door   dog

5. This is for telling time.

   climb   clock   clear

6. This one is an animal.

   road   race   rabbit

7. You wear this.

   shoe   shape   ship

8. It is wet.

   read   race   rain

9

Riddles

Write the answer to each riddle.
Find the word you need in the box.

car	rope	pencil
fish	teeth	ice cream

1. It is long and yellow. You write with it.

   It is a _____ .

2. You can ride in it. It has four wheels.

   It is a _____ .

3. It swims in a bowl. The color may be gold.

   It is a _____ .

4. It is long and thin. You jump with it.

   It is a _____ .

5. You use them for eating. You brush them.

   They are _____ .

6. It is cold and sweet. You eat it. It is

   _____ .

Pick the Right Word

Choose the correct word from the box for each sentence. Write the word on the line.

six	said	fun

. There are _____ red pencils.

. We had _____ at the party.

. Mother _____ we could go.

play	find	big

. That is a _____ drum.

. Will you _____ ball?

. I cannot _____ my book.

try	sad	what

. That boy looks _____ .

. _____ did you say?

. Let's _____ the new slide.

e Homework Booklet ©1983, Instructional Fair, Inc.

Comparing Words

Circle the word that fits in the sentence.

1. A pencil is _____ than a log.

   bigger   thinner   thicker

2. A pan is _____ than a tub.

   smaller   higher   bigger

3. A bonfire is _____ than a match.

   thinner   smaller   hotter

4. A pail is _____ than a glass.

   smaller   better   bigger

5. A house is _____ than a car.

   lower   higher   finer

6. An ice cube is _____ than a fire.

   warmer   nicer   colder

7. Cotton is _____ than wood.

   softer   harder   safer

8. A bang is _____ than a hiss.

   softer   harder   louder

12

More Than One!

Circle <u>all</u> the words that could fit in the space and make sense.

1. I like to hear a funny _____ .

   joke   smile   story   song

2. In our garden we grew _____ .

   cookies   corn   beans   butter

3. When it is _____ , we turn on the light.

   dark   night   sound   another

4. I'll be there in one _____ .

   second   hour   point   minute

5. We heard her _____ way over here.

   think   yell   shout   laugh

6. That sure is a _____ river.

   wide   long   deep   ready

13

More Than One!

Circle __all__ the words that could fit in the space and make sense.

1. We saw the boys were ready to

   _____ .

   fight   race   sorry   answer

2. Then we heard a _____ noise.

   shape   loud   second   pretty

3. I want that coat because it's _____ .

   soft   surprise   better   different

4. There were _____ red bikes at school.

   many   four   seven   tree

5. We went to the fire station _____ school.

   still   after   before   again

6. The children raced up the _____ .

   hill   game   steps   street

14

©1983, Instructional Fair, I

More Than One!

Circle **all** the words that could fit in the space and make sense.

1. A _____ can climb a tree.

   cat   boy   shoe   town

2. A _____ makes a good pet.

   store   kitten   friend   duck

3. A _____ is good to eat.

   cookie   dress   chicken   farm

4. It is fun to play in the _____.

   fight   snow   park   water

5. You can put on a _____.

   shoe   drop   coat   shirt

15

A Trip to the Zoo

Circle __all__ the words that could fit in the space and make sense.

1. We will go to the zoo _____ .

   today　　other　　tomorrow　　time

2. To get there, we had to go _____ the bridge.

   over　　early　　around　　enough

3. First we went to see the _____ lions.

   empty　　angry　　large　　lazy

4. We couldn't believe how _____ the elephants were!

   huge　　friendly　　leave　　hungry

5. We learned that giraffes can't make any _____ .

   sound　　neck　　noise　　tall

16

What Happens Next?

Circle the phrase that best completes each sentence.

1. I thought I heard something so _____ .

    I listened carefully.
    I climbed the fence.

2. I was so scared that _____ .
    I couldn't move.
    I wanted supper.

3. It kept coming _____ .

    around and slow.
    closer and closer.

4. Then it landed _____ .

    right on top of me.
    without waiting for it.

5. It was only my dog Lick who _____ .
    brought his doll with him.
    wanted to sleep with me.

17

What Happens Next?

Circle the phrase that best completes each sentence.

1. We went to visit _____.

> our next door neighbor.
> your ugly ladder.

2. We knocked _____.

> on the door.
> under the dish.

3. Then we heard a _____.

> heavy smell.
> very loud roar.

4. A lion _____.

> climbed up the clock.
> opened the door.

5. It was only Beth wearing _____!

> an empty basket!
> a Halloween mask!

18

©1983, Instructional Fair, Inc

The Elephant

Check (X) the phrase that best completes each sentence.

1. "Mom! There's an elephant _____!"
   _____ in our backyard!"
   _____ under my peanut butter!"

2. "Oh, Kay, I'm not dumb enough to _____ ."
   _____ wonder why you're so unhappy."
   _____ believe a story like that."

3. "I'm not joking. I'm _____ ."
   _____ getting ready for bed."
   _____ telling the truth."

4. Just then we heard a knock _____ .
   _____ above the picnic basket.
   _____ at our front door.

5. A man said, "Lady, an elephant _____ ."
   _____ got away from the circus."
   _____ climbed a tall ladder."

19

 ©1983, Instructional Fair, Inc.

Which Make Sense?

Underline __all__ the phrases that make sense.

Mother and I like to _____ .

> eat lunch in the river.
> bake cupcakes together.
> tell each other strange dreams.
> fly around the kitchen.
> watch a long parade.
> skate on the sidewalk.

It scares me when _____ .

> I have a bad dream.
> I fall out of bed.
> I see a pretty picture.
> a car runs over a dog.
> a big dog barks at me.
> it sends in the corner.

20

Which Make Sense?

Underline <u>all</u> the phrases that make sense.

Tomorrow morning we will _____ .

find the lost ball.
take another cough drop.
have a surprise party.
stay in the window.
teach the duck to bark.
plant a beautiful dress.

That new ball _____ .

fits in my pocket.
jumped over the mouse.
was a real surprise.
bounces as high as a house.
is made of nothing.
got dropped in the paint.

21

 ©1983, Instructional Fair, Inc.

What Can Animals Do?

Underline <u>all</u> the phrases that can make sense.

A kitten can _____ .

play in the grass.
ride a little car.
bark like a dog.
laugh and cry.
walk and run.
sleep on a chair.

A bird can _____ .

fly like an airplane.
eat food.
be a pet.
build a school.
make a cake.
live in a tree.

What Would You See?

Underline __all__ the phrases that can make sense.

At the farm we saw ——————— .

a big green tractor.
a lost shoe store.
some fat pigs.
many white chickens.
four brown cows.
a long barn.

At a party we saw ——————— .

a bright star.
a pretty birthday cake.
funny hats.
some big balloons.
lots of happy children.
three sleeping feet.

23

©1983, Instructional Fair, Inc.

Puzzle Sentences

Fill in the spaces with the right word from the Helper Box.

Helper Box		
choose	suit	face
heavy	finish	quiet

1. I will wear my new swim _____.

2. He fell flat on his _____.

3. "I _____ Pat for my side," said Ted.

4. "Shhh. Be very _____," said Kay.

5. This box is too _____ for me to carry.

6. Beth was the first one across the _____ line.

1.
2.
3.
4.
5.
6.

24

Working Hard

Fill in the spaces with the right word from the Helper Box.

Helper Box		
stand	clean	save
wash	earn	shovel

1. I work to _____ money.

2. Sometimes I _____ the car.

3. Or I _____ up my room.

4. In winter I _____ snow.

5. Once I had a lemonade _____.

6. I spend some of my money and I _____ some.

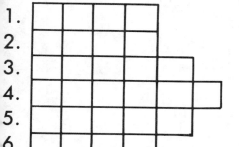

1.
2.
3.
4.
5.
6.

Hide and Seek

Fill in the spaces with the right word from the Helper Box.

Helper Box

ask	games	find
over	found	under

1. I like to play _____ with my friend.

2. She will hide and I try to _____ her.

3. She got _____ the bed.

4. I looked all _____ for her.

5. I had to _____ Daddy to help me find her.

6. We _____ her when she laughed.

1.
2.
3.
4.
5.
6.

26

The Yellow Birds

Read the words in the box. Write the correct word where it fits in the story.

grass	mother	yellow	nest	eat
eggs	found	babies	made	food

The Baby Birds

Two little _____ birds wanted to build a _____ . They looked for _____ and leaves. When they _____ some grass, they flew away with it. Then they _____ it into a nest.

The _____ bird laid some eggs. Soon there were three _____ . The little ones wanted to _____ all the time. The big birds were busy bringing them _____ .

27

The Little Dragon

Write the missing words. Use the words under each paragraph.

I couldn't _____ my eyes.

_____ the door was a little dragon.

"Help me," it said. "I'm _____."

lost   believe   behind

"Where did you come _____?"
I asked. "How did you get _____?
And why are you so _____?"

from   small   here

"It's a long _____," the dragon
said. "I was doing a magic _____
when all of a sudden something went
_____."

wrong   story   trick

28

Flying High

Write the missing words. Use the words under each paragraph.

I dreamed I could _____ . I flew

_____ above the earth. Cars looked

like little _____ .

high   ants   fly

I flew _____ clouds. I landed on

a tall _____ . People stopped and

_____ me.

watched   over   building

I took off _____ . Zoom! An

airplane _____ hit me. Then I

_____ up.

again   almost   woke

29

The Baby Bear

Write the missing words. Use the words under each paragraph.

One summer day, we were having a _____ in the woods. By a big _____ was a baby _____ .

tree　　　　bear　　　　color　　　　picnic

"Come _____ , little bear," Joe called. "I want to _____ you home for a _____ ."

take　　　　forgot　　　　here　　　　pet

Just then we _____ a loud growl. It was the little cub's _____ . "I was just kidding," said Joe. "I already have too _____ pets at home."

mother　　　　many　　　　heard　　　　until

Creamed Corn for Supper

Write the missing words. Use the words under each paragraph.

"Creamed corn? I _____ eat it,"

said Sue. "It will make me _____ up.

May I have _____ else?"

can't   throw   might   something

Dad said, "It will help you grow big and

_____ . It's _____ for you.

And we don't have anything _____ ."

easy   else   good   strong

I accidentally knocked the _____

of corn off the _____ . "Did you

_____ to do that?" roared Dad.

table   bowl   plant   mean

31

Hide and Seek

Write the missing words. Use the words under the story.

At the birthday _____, we

played hide and _____. They

couldn't _____ me at all.

| find | party | lost | seek |

Can you _____ where I was

_____ ? I hid _____ the door.

| behind | should | guess | hiding |

_____ I was "it", I _____

everyone in a _____.

| forgot | hurry | When | found |

The Brown Squirrel

Write the missing words. Use the words under the story.

A little brown _____ ran up,

grabbed the _____ and raced back

to its _____ in the tree.

| peanut | bone | squirrel | hole |

He's storing _____. When

there's snow on the ground this _____,

he'll have _____ to eat.

| near | enough | winter | food |

Squirrels have to _____ for their

food. They can't _____ it at a

_____ .

| buy | store | hunt | glad |

33

A Snow Child

Some words are missing from the story. Use the words from the box to finish the story.

slush	sleep	clear	snow
	slide	climb	
stop	smaller	stand	slip

A Snow Child

Once upon a time there was a child made from _____. He could not run or _____ up on things. He could only _____ and _____ along. At night he would _____ moving. He had to _____ standing up.

On one _____, warm day he began to turn to _____. Then he could not _____ up very well anymore. He became _____ and smaller. And one day he was all gone.

One Too Many

In each sentence, one word doesn't belong. Circle it. The first one is done for you.

1. We were going to paint a (try) picture.

2. "I will paint the when sun yellow," I said.

3. Bob said, "I will paint the grass green very."

4. "Let's make it where different and funny," said Ann.

5. "Put a tree in the should sky," she said.

6. "And off put a house on the sun," I laughed.

7. "Let's give it to now our teacher," said Bob.

35

Silly Animals

In each sentence, one word doesn't belong. Circle it. The first one is done for you.

1. Did you see the goat in (thing) the boat?

2. What is fine that dragon doing in my wagon?

3. Did you know a fish can what make a wish?

4. Who will help a bear build a which chair?

5. I can't nothing believe a fox is in the box!

6. Whoever saw flower kittens wearing mittens?

7. Is that our but dog in the hollow log?

One Too Many

In each sentence, one word doesn't belong. Circle it. The first one is done for you.

1. A bee got into our (away) house.

2. "How do you those catch a bee?" I asked.

3. "It can hurt you!" said never Mom.

4. "Duck!" said Mom. "Here better it comes again."

5. "Get me a paper to which hit it with," said Mom.

6. Just then the bee flew every out the open door.

37

One Too Many

In each sentence, one word doesn't belong. Circle it.

1. I ran and jumped into the (sure) swimming pool.

2. The water was just short right, good and warm.

3. "Come on leave in!" I yelled. "The water's fine."

4. We swam to the between deep end.

5. We took turns jumping dirty off the diving board.

6. At last Mom said, "We luck must go now."

What's the Word?

Carefully read each sentence. Think what the underlined word means. Circle the picture that shows what the word is.

1. Dan's father is a <u>barber</u> who cuts hair.

2. He uses a pair of sharp <u>scissors</u>.

3. For children, he puts a <u>board</u> across the chair arms.

4. Then he covers them with a <u>sheet</u>.

5. When he is through, he gives them a <u>lollipop</u> to lick.

39

What's the Word?

Carefully read each sentence. Think what the underlined word means. Circle the picture that shows what the word is.

1. Slowly from the sky came the huge <u>spaceship.</u>

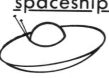  

2. Out came not a person but a <u>robot.</u>

3. I ran to the <u>telephone</u> to call the police.

4. Then I got my <u>camera</u> to take a picture.

5. But there was no <u>film</u> in the camera!

40

What's the Word?

Carefully read each sentence. Think what the underlined word means. Circle the picture that shows what the word is.

1. The cowboy threw a <u>lasso</u> around the horse's neck.

2. Then he put the <u>saddle</u> on the horse.

3. Next he put a gun into his <u>holster</u>.

4. He put his foot into the <u>stirrup</u> and swung up.

5. Suddenly the horse <u>reared</u> straight up.

41

What's the Word?

Carefully read each sentence. Think what the underlined word means. Circle the picture that shows what the word is.

1. Tim cuts the grass with a <u>lawnmower</u>.

2. He puts the cut grass into a <u>garbage</u> <u>bag</u>.

3. In the fall he will <u>rake</u> up leaves.

Looking good!

4. He is saving his money to buy a <u>motorcycle</u>.

You have finished

Step 1

42

TUTOR'S GUIDE
Reading Level 2

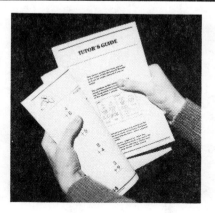

This answer section has been placed in the center of this Homework Booklet so it can be easily removed if you so desire.

The solutions in this manual reflect the layout of the exercises to simplify checking.

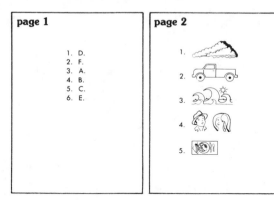

page 1

1. D.
2. F.
3. A.
4. B.
5. C.
6. E.

page 2

1.
2.
3.
4.
5.

A motivational award is provided on the inside back cover. It has been designed to be signed by the tutor, either a parent or teacher.

Motivational suggestion: After the student completes each step, mark the achievement by placing a sticker next to that step shown on the award.

Solutions

page 3
1. C.
2. D.
3. E.
4. B.
5. A.

page 4
1. E.
2. D.
3. F.
4. C.
5. A.

page 5
1. bike
2. fast
3. races
4. money
5. sister

page 6
1. truck
2. street
3. water
4. house
5. baby

page 7
1. doll
2. dress
3. careful
4. brother
5. ago

page 8
1. bank
2. guns
3. chase
4. caught
5. dollars

page 9
1. chair
2. boat
3. house
4. dog
5. clock
6. rabbit
7. shoe
8. rain

page 10
1. pencil
2. car
3. fish
4. rope
5. teeth
6. ice cream

page 11
1. six
2. fun
3. said
4. big
5. play
6. find
7. sad
8. what
9. try

page 12
1. thinner
2. smaller
3. hotter
4. bigger
5. higher
6. colder
7. softer
8. louder

page 13
1. joke   story   song
2. corn   beans
3. dark   night
4. second   hour   minute
5. yell   shout   laugh
6. wide   long   deep

page 14
1. fight   race   answer
2. loud   second
3. soft   better   different
4. many   four   seven
5. after   before
6. hill   steps   street

1. cat   boy
2. kitten   duck
3. cookie   chicken
4. snow   park   water
5. shoe   coat   shirt

1. today   tomorrow
2. over   around
3. angry   large   lazy
4. huge   friendly hungry
5. sound   noise

1. I listened carefully.
2. I couldn't move.
3. closer and closer.
4. right on top of me.
5. wanted to sleep with me.

1. our next door neighbor.
2. on the door.
3. very loud roar.
4. opened the door.
5. a Halloween mask!

1. X in our backyard!"
2. X believe a story like that."
3. X telling the truth."
4. X at our front door.
5. X got away from the circus."

bake cupcakes together.
tell each other strange dreams.
watch a long parade.
skate on the sidewalk.

I have a bad dream.
I fall out of bed.
a car runs over a dog.
a big dog barks at me.

find the lost ball.
take another cough drop.
have a surprise party.

fits in my pocket.
was a real surprise.
bounces as high as a house.
got dropped in the paint.

play in the grass.
walk and run.
sleep on a chair.

fly like an airplane.
eat food.
be a pet.
live in a tree.

a big green tractor.
some fat pigs.
many white chickens.
four brown cows.
a long barn.

a pretty birthday cake.
funny hats.
some big balloons.
lots of happy children.

1. suit
2. face
3. choose
4. quiet
5. heavy
6. finish

1. earn
2. wash
3. clean
4. shovel
5. stand
6. save

1. games
2. find
3. under
4. over
5. ask
6. found

Solutions

Solutions

page 27

yellow
nest
grass
found
made
mother
babies
eat
food

page 28

believe
Behind
lost

from
here
small

story
trick
wrong

page 29

fly
high
ants

over
building
watched

again
almost
woke

page 30

picnic
tree
bear

here
take
pet

heard
mother
many

page 31

can't
throw
something

strong
good
else

bowl
table
mean

page 32

party
seek
find

guess
hiding
behind

When
found
hurry

page 33

squirrel
peanut
hole

food
winter
enough

hunt
buy
store

page 34

snow
climb
slip
slide
stop
sleep
clear
slush
stand
smaller

page 35

1. try
2. when
3. very
4. where
5. should
6. off
7. now

page 36

1. thing
2. fine
3. what
4. which
5. nothing
6. flower
7. but

page 37

1. away
2. those
3. never
4. better
5. which
6. every

page 38

1. sure
2. short
3. leave
4. between
5. dirty
6. luck

page 39

1.
2.
3.
4.
5.

page 40

1.
2.
3.
4.
5.

page 41

1.
2.
3.
4.
5.

page 42

1.
2.
3.
4.

page 43

1. from
2. name
3. late
4. left
5. dear
6. spot

page 44

1. ten
2. eat
3. saw
4. not
5. now
6. owl
7. end

page 45

stick	ground
pool	walk
pail	year
drink	string
strong	well

page 46

1. tray
   gray
2. trash
   crash
3. cry
   try
4. dream
   cream
5. drip
   trip

page 47

1. show
2. near
3. play
4. fly
5. game
6. tree
7. sky
8. cat

page 48

1. sea
2. me
3. elf
4. shelf
5. far
6. star
7. pail
8. sail

page 49

1. rock
   rock
2. cut
   cut
3. list
   list
4. talk
   talk
5. smoke
   smoke

page 50

Don't (point) the gun at me.

His house is next to an empty (lot.)

They will (ship) the elephant by train.

Who wrote this nice (letter) to you?

page 51

1. horse
2. very
3. will
4. live
5. Where
6. guess

page 52

1. alone
2. noise
3. know
4. Then
5. want
6. father

page 53

1. where
2. lost
3. new
4. must
5. same
6. think

page 54

1. party
2. children
3. track
4. sing
5. bought
6. more

page 55

5
3
1
4
2

page 56

1. friend
2. story
3. began
4. can

5. go
6. cut
7. rock
8. talk

page 57

1. leave
2. say
3. place
4. do
5. question
6. nice
7. leap
8. have

page 58

1. large
2. look
3. nice
4. choose
5. away
6. tall
7. cold
8. glad

page 59

1. make
2. too
3. start
4. hold

5. home
6. no
7. by
8. over

page 60

1. back
2. got
3. much
4. low

5. old
6. here
7. down
8. end

page 61

1. sad   leave
2. no   wet

3. walk   slow
4. few   short

5. none   strong
6. down   under

page 62

1. off
2. my
3. out
4. that

5. under
6. night
7. come
8. less

page 63

1. new
2. walk
3. in
4. play
5. then
6. lose
7. all
8. big

page 64

1. meat
2. one
3. two
4. so
5. do
6. be

page 65

hear — sea
see — here
meet ——— meat

for — buy
pear — four
by — pair

son — cent
sent — so
sew — sun

dear — knew
new — deer
fair ——— fare

page 66

1. peace
2. blue
3. heal
4. sun
5. ball
6. bear
7. herd

page 67

I will (train) my dog to sit up.

Bill may go to the (head) of the line.

She will (rock) the baby to sleep.

Please (hand) me the book.

page 68

I got all of them (right.)

We saw them dig gold from a (mine.)

Dad was angry to see the flat (tire.)

We helped (plant) a tree yesterday.

page 69

1. into
2. Baseball
3. birthday
4. sidewalk
5. something
6. armchair
7. houseboat
8. pancake

page 70

1. schoolyard
2. mailman
3. bluejay
4. grapefruit
5. goldfish
6. toothbrush
7. grandfather
8. popcorn

page 71

1. man
2. fire
3. fireman

4. wind
5. mill
6. windmill

7. play
8. ground
9. playground

page 72

page 73

1. bike
2. moon
3. cookies
4. car
5. mitten
6. whale

page 74

Answers will vary.

Solutions

page 75

The frog has glasses on.
The goat and the pig are dancing.

page 76

The dog has an umbrella.
The bug has a hat on.

page 77

1. door
2. fish
3. rock
4. ball
5. goat
6. picture
7. hot
8. beans
9. corn
10. inch

page 78

1. vowels
2. wheel
3. snake
4. blocks
5. butterfly
6. dragon

page 79

1. T
2. F
3. T
4. F
5. F
6. T
7. T
8. F

page 80

1. T
2. F
3. F
4. T
5. F
6. F
7. F
8. T
9. T
10. F
11. F
12. T

page 81

Little Red Hen was afraid.
Rosa was happy.
Sam was sad.

page 82

Bill was sad.
Maria was happy.
Ray and Tom were afraid.

page 83

bird
garden

page 84

kite
barn

page 85

A Soap Boat
The Little Lost Kitten

page 86

The New Tree House
Fun At The Park

recombining letters

Change-Around Letters

Look at the underlined word in each sentence. Then find the word in the box that has the same letters as the underlined word. Write the new word on the line. The first one is done for you.

dear	from	name
late	left	spot

1. The box ____from____ Uncle Joe has a square <u>form</u>.

2. What does your _____ <u>mean?</u>

3. If you read that <u>tale</u> now, you'll be _____.

4. He _____ his <u>felt</u> hat on the chair.

5. My _____ friend just <u>read</u> a new book.

6. <u>Stop!</u> You'll make a _____ on the rug.

The Homework Booklet ©1983, Instructional Fair, Inc.

Change-Around Letters

Look at the underlined word in each sentence. Then find the word in the box that has the same letters as the underlined word. Write the new word on the line. The first one is done for you.

ten	saw	owl	eat
end	not	now	

1. The fish was in the <u>net</u>.
   Can you count to ___ten___ ?

2. Have you ever tasted <u>tea</u>?
   The food will soon be ready to _____ .

3. Where <u>was</u> the cute little kitten found?
   We _____ many things on our trip.

4. A <u>ton</u> is very heavy.
   No, we can _____ go.

5. Who <u>won</u> the race?
   Is it time to go _____ ?

6. That table is very <u>low</u>.
   The _____ hunts for food at night.

7. The fox lives in a <u>den</u>.
   How did the story _____ ?

44

Silly Poems

Make a silly rhyme by writing the right word in the line.

Quick, quick hand me a _____ .

  stick   top

I heard a sound in the _____ .

  ground   house

I wish our school had a _____ .

  flag   pool

Let us talk while we _____ .

  walk   shout

The dog's tail was in a _____ .

  dish   pail

I couldn't hear for half a _____ .

  day   year

I think, I think I need a _____ .

  dollar drink

Will you bring the ball of _____ .

  string snow

To sing that song you must be _____ .

  unhappy strong

The little bell fell in the _____ .

  well   water

45

Rhyming Words

Find and write a word from the box that fits each phrase. The words in each pair of phrases should have all the letters alike except the first one.

dream   drip   cry   trip   try
cream   gray   tray   crash   trash

1. carry food on a _____

   a color is _____

2. take out the _____

   have a _____

3. hear baby _____

   you can _____

4. at night I _____

   eat ice _____

5. water may _____

   go on a _____

46

Rhyming

Choose a word from the box that rhymes with the underlined word, then write it on the line.

| near | fly | show | play |

1. Here we <u>go</u> to the _____ .

2. The little <u>deer</u> came quite _____ .

3. Every <u>day</u> we ride and _____ .

4. Tell me <u>why</u> you can't _____ .

| sky | game | tree | cat |

5. Who <u>came</u> to play the _____ ?

6. What did you <u>see</u> up in the _____ ?

7. The bird flew <u>by</u> up in the _____ ?

8. Did you say <u>that</u> you saw the _____ ?

47

Rhyming

Circle the words in each box that rhyme. Then write the rhyming words on the blank lines to complete the sentence. The first one is done for you.

(me)   star   (sea)

1. The fish in the _____sea_____,
2. cannot catch ___me___.

egg   shelf   elf

3. See the little _____,
4. sitting on the _____.

far   fan   star

5. Way up in the sky so _____,
6. we see a little shining _____.

pail   said   sail

7. Put some water in the _____,
8. where our little boat will _____.

48

Use It Twice

Complete each pair of sentences by using the same word from the box <u>twice</u>. The first one is done for you.

talk	list	rock
cut	smoke	

1. The baby's bed can _____ rock _____ .
   There is a _____ rock _____ in my shoe.

2. Please _____ the cake.
   Lois has a _____ on her knee.

3. I have a _____ of good books to read.
   Would you please _____ the things we need?

4. Mr. Jones and Rob had a _____ about airplanes.
   Don't _____ during the program.

5. Don't _____ that cigarette.
   Where there's _____, there's fire.

49

Which One?

The underlined words are spelled the same but have different meanings. One meaning is given above the sentences. Circle the underlined word with that meaning.

turn straight to; aim
1. The <u>point</u> of the pin is sharp.
2. Don't <u>point</u> the gun at me.

piece of land
1. His house is next to an empty <u>lot</u>.
2. She has a <u>lot</u> of stuffed animals.

send
1. They will <u>ship</u> the elephant by train.
2. We saw the <u>ship</u> way out in the sea.

mail
1. What <u>letter</u> comes before Z?
2. Who wrote this nice <u>letter</u> to you?

50

Look Alike Words

Read each sentence carefully. Look carefully at the words below each sentence. Write the missing word.

1. I want to ride the brown _____ .

   horse   house

2. I would be _____ happy if I had a horse.

   very   every

3. But I _____ never own one.

   well   will   wall

4. We _____ in a town.

   like   live

5. _____ would we keep a horse in town?

   Where   Were

6. I _____ I'll be happy with my bike.

   grass   guess

51

Look Alike Words

Read each sentence carefully. Look carefully at the words below each sentence. Write the missing word.

1. Penny was _____ in the house.

   alone   along

2. She heard a funny _____ .

   nose   noise

3. "I don't _____ what that was," she said.

   knew   know

4. _____ she heard it again.

   Them   Then

5. "I don't _____ to be alone any more," she said.

   want   went

6. Just then her _____ walked in.

   feather   father

52

Look Alike Words

Read each sentence carefully. Look carefully at the words below each sentence. Write the missing word.

1. I wonder _____ my yellow race car is?

   where   when

2. I hope it isn't _____ .

   last   lost

3. It's a _____ toy and I like it a lot.

   now   new

4. I _____ have left it at Bob's house.

   most   must

5. Bob and I like the _____ toys.

   same   some

6. I _____ I'll see if he found it.

   think   thank

53

Look Alike Words

Read each sentence carefully. Look carefully at the words below each sentence. Write the missing word.

1. I'm going to Patty's birthday _____ .

   pretty   party

2. There will be seven other _____ there.

   children   chicken

3. I got her some _____ for her train set.

   truck   track   trick

4. First we'll _____ "Happy Birthday, Patty."

   sing   sign

5. Then she'll open the presents we _____ at the store.

   brought   bought

6. Then I'll ask for some _____ of that great cake!

   more   move

54

Finding Meanings of Words

Read each sentence. Then find the meaning of the underlined word in the list below. Write the number of the sentence next to the meaning. The first one is done for you.

1. The <u>cover</u> for the jar was gone.

2. The air was cold and <u>still</u>.

3. The <u>river</u> was full after the rain.

4. We have <u>never</u> visited there.

5. Yours will be the <u>next</u> report, Jan.

_____ the one following

_____ long, narrow body of water

__1__ an object that goes over something

_____ not ever; not at any time

_____ to be quiet; not move

On to step 3

You have finished

Step 2

55

Words That Mean the Same

Find a word in the box which means about the <u>same</u> as the underlined word in each sentence. Then write the word on the blank line.

Begin Step 3

can	story	friend	began

1. _____ I have a new <u>pal</u> at school.

2. _____ The <u>tale</u> the teacher read to us was fun.

3. _____ We <u>started</u> the project in the morning.

4. _____ They <u>are able</u> to finish in a short time.

cut	talk	go	rock

5. _____ May I <u>leave</u> now?

6. _____ <u>Slice</u> the apple before you eat it.

7. _____ There was a large <u>stone</u> in the street.

8. _____ She can <u>say</u> a lot in a short time.

56

Words with the Same Meaning

Circle the word on the right that means the <u>same</u> as the word on the left. The first one is done for you.

1. go   gave
                  (leave)

2. tell   say
                  tale

3. put   place
                  take

4. act   walk
                  do

5. ask   question
                  answer

6. kind   some
                  nice

7. jump   run
                  leap

8. own   have
                  our

57

Words That Mean the Same

Circle one of the words on the right that means the <u>same</u> as the word on the left. The first one is done for you.

1. big   (large)
                  black

2. see   said
                  look

3. good   nice
                  gate

4. pick   lock
                  choose

5. gone   away
                  along

6. high   talk
                  tall

7. cool   cold
                  cart

8. happy   sad
                  glad

Words That Mean the Same

Find a word in the box that means about the <u>same</u> as the underlined word in each sentence. Then write the word on the line.

too	start	make	hold

1. _____ We can <u>build</u> a house of blocks.
2. _____ Pete is going to the store <u>also</u>.
3. _____ The new class will soon <u>begin</u>.
4. _____ <u>Kee</u>p that pencil for now.

over	no	home	by

5. _____ Our <u>house</u> is painted white.
6. _____ There were <u>not any</u> cookies left.
7. _____ Do you live <u>near</u> the railroad tracks?
8. _____ The light pole is just <u>above</u> the bush.

59

Opposites

Find a word in the box that means the <u>opposite</u> of the underlined word in each sentence. Write the word on the blank line.

back	got	low	much

1. _____ They came in the <u>front</u> door.

2. _____ We <u>gave away</u> two little ducks today.

3. _____ There is <u>little</u> left to be done.

4. _____ That chair is very <u>high.</u>

old	end	down	here

5. _____ The lady in the play was <u>young</u>.

6. _____ Over <u>there</u> you will find the paper.

7. _____ He went <u>up</u> the ladder.

8. _____ Let's <u>begin</u> this right now.

60

More Opposites

Choose a word from the box that is the <u>opposite</u> of each underlined word. Then write it on the line.

sad	wet	leave	no

1. I am <u>happy</u> that you must <u>stay</u>.

_____   _____

2. <u>Yes</u>, the clothes are <u>dry</u>.

_____   _____

slowly	few	walk	short

3. Can you <u>run</u> <u>fast</u>?

_____   _____

4. <u>Many</u> dresses are <u>long</u>.

_____   _____

strong	under	none	down

5. Are <u>all</u> of these ropes <u>weak</u>?

_____   _____

6. Did the ball go <u>up</u> and <u>over</u> the bridge?

_____   _____

61

Opposites

Find a word in the box that means the opposite of the underlined word in each sentence. Then write the word on the line.

out	off	that	my

1. _____ Did you have the light turned <u>on</u>?

2. _____ <u>Your</u> new ball will be fun to play with.

3. _____ She went <u>in</u> the back door.

4. _____ What do you think of <u>this</u> game?

less	night	come	under

5. _____ The ball went <u>over</u> the fence.

6. _____ The <u>day</u> of the parade was clear and warm.

7. _____ When will you <u>go</u> to the park?

8. _____ Are there <u>more</u> than six pencils left?

62

Opposites

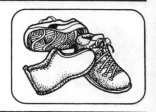

Circle the word on the right that means the __opposite__ of the word on the left. The first one is done for you.

1. old   (new)
                 good

2. run   hide
                 walk

3. out   for
                 in

4. work   try
                 play

5. now   next
                 then

6. find   lose
                 found

7. part   all
                 tall

8. small   little
                 big

63

Words That Sound the Same

Each pair of sentences contains two words that sound the same but are spelled differently. One of the two words is already underlined. Find and circle the second word. The first one is done for you.

1. <u>Meet</u> me at seven o'clock.
   I'll bring the (meat) for supper.

2. I <u>won</u> a nice prize.
   But I missed the grand prize by one point.

3. The shells were <u>too</u> few.
   I found two shells in the water.

4. My mother taught me to <u>sew.</u>
   It was so good of you to come.

5. The grass was covered with <u>dew</u>.
   I can't do much when the grass is wet.

6. There is a <u>bee</u> hive in our yard.
   Can it be full of honey?

Which Words Sound Alike?

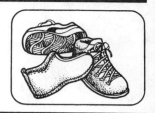

Draw a line between the words in each box that <u>sound</u> the same but are not <u>spelled</u> the same. The first one is done for you.

hear	sea
see	here
meet	meat

for	buy
pear	four
by	pair

son	cent
sent	so
sew	sun

dear	knew
new	deer
fair	fare

65

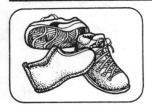

Words That Sound the Same

Each pair of sentences contains two words that sound the same, but are spelled differently. One of the two words is already underlined. Find and circle the second word. The first one is done for you.

1. The mouse took a <u>piece</u> of cake. He took it home to eat in (peace.)

2. The wind <u>blew</u> the clouds away. Then the sky was blue.

3. John tripped and hurt his <u>heel</u>. It took a long time to heal.

4. The father woke his <u>son</u> up early. They went out to see the sun come up.

5. There is no need to <u>bawl</u>. I will give you your ball.

6. These are the <u>bare</u> facts. There is a bear outside the door.

7. I <u>heard</u> a sound. It is a herd of animals.

66

Which One?

The underlined words are spelled the same but have different meanings. One meaning is given above the sentences. Circle the underlined word with that meaning.

teach
1. I will <u>train</u> my dog to sit up.
2. Jim took a ride on a <u>train.</u>

front
1. A hat will keep your <u>head</u> warm.
2. Bill may go to the <u>head</u> of the line.

move back and forth
1. He threw a <u>rock</u> at the window.
2. She will <u>rock</u> the baby to sleep.

give
1. Please <u>hand</u> me the book.
2. One clock <u>hand</u> is gone.

67

Which One?

The underlined words are spelled the same but have different meanings. One meaning is given above the sentences. Circle the underlined word with that meaning.

not wrong
1. I got all of them right.
2. Go to the corner and turn right.

hole in the ground
1. We saw them dig gold from a mine.
2. That toy is mine, not yours.

wheel
1. Too much running will tire you out.
2. Dad was angry to see the flat tire.

put in the ground
1. We helped plant a tree yesterday.
2. I gave Mother a flower plant for her birthday.

68

Compound Words

A compound word is two words written as one. Write the correct compound word from the box in the sentence where it fits.

something	birthday	pancake
houseboat	into	sidewalk
armchair	baseball	

1. The dog went _____ his house.

2. _____ is a game.

3. Allen had a _____ party.

4. We have a _____ in front of our house.

5. There is _____ in the box.

6. She is sitting in an _____ .

7. Some people live on a _____ .

8. A _____ is a good thing to eat.

69

Compounds

Two words together make a compound word. Choose one word from line one and one word from line two to make a compound word that goes with the word on the left. The first one is done for you.

> 1. grape mail school blue gold
> 2. jay yard fish fruit man

1. play here	schoolyard

2. person   _____

3. bird   _____

4. eat it   _____

5. it swims   _____

> 1. grand pop tooth
> 2. corn brush father

6. it cleans   _____

7. a person   _____

8. eat it   _____

70

Make a Compound

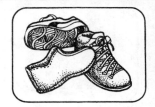

Write a word from the box in each of the first two sentences. Then combine the two words to make one word (a compound word) and write it in the third sentence.

fire	man

1. That _____ was working at a house.

2. There was a big _____ .

3. The man was a _____ .

wind	mill

4. The _____ was blowing hard.

5. The farmer owned a _____ .

6. The _____ helped in the farmer's work.

play	ground

7. We _____ here after school.

8. You can plant seeds in the _____ .

9. A _____ is a place for fun.

Keep up the good work

You have finished

Step 3

71

Can You Do This?

Mark the picture according to the directions.

bed   donkey   nickel

tent   blanket   roof

Reading Skills

Begin Step 4

1. Find the bed. Put a circle around it.
2. Put two lines under the tent.
3. Put an X on the blanket.
4. Find the picture of a nickel. Put a circle around it.
5. Put a line under the roof.
6. Find the donkey. Put a line over the donkey.

72

Can You Do This?

Mark the picture according to the directions.

1. Put a red X on something you ride on.

2. Put a blue X on something that is in the sky.

3. Put a yellow X on something good to eat.

4. Put a black X on something you ride in.

5. Put an orange X on something you put on your hand.

6. Put a green X on something that lives in the water.

whale

bike

mitten

cookies

car

moon

73

Can You Do This?

Get a piece of paper. Then draw a picture according to the directions.

1. Make a big house.

2. Put three windows in the house.

3. Put a red door in the house.

4. Color the house blue.

5. Make two trees beside the house.

6. Color them green.

7. Make red and yellow flowers in front of the house.

8. Make a sun in the sky.

74

Is It Funny?

Underline the sentence that answers the question.

What is funny about this?

The frog has four legs.

The frog has glasses on.

A frog is green.

What is funny about this?

The goat has horns.

The pig has ears.

The goat and the pig are dancing.

75

Is It Funny?

Underline the sentence that answers the question.

What is funny about this?

It is raining outside.

The dog has an umbrella.

The umbrella is black.

What is funny about this?

The bug is outside.

The grass is green.

The bug has a hat on.

76

One Too Many!

Circle the word that does not belong.

1. clown   door   elephant   lion

2. fish   duck   bird   chicken

3. star   moon   sun   rock

4. swim   ball   ride   run

5. sad   happy   goat   angry

6. picture   penny   nickel   quarter

7. winter   hot   cold   freeze

8. cookies   cake   beans   ice cream

9. banana   corn   apple   orange

10. inch   week   month   year

77

What Is It?

Look at the pictures. Then write the correct word in front of the description.

snake butterfly wheel

blocks dragon vowels

1. _____ We each have two sounds. We help you learn to read.

2. _____ I am round. A wagon could not go without me.

3. _____ I am an animal, but I do not have any legs.

4. _____ We are square. Children like to make houses with us.

5. _____ I am very pretty. I have wings and I fly.

6. _____ People are afraid of me! I breathe fire and smoke.

True or False Time

Write a T beside the statement if it is true
and an F if the statement is false.

1. The snow is cold. _____

2. A pig can fly in the sky. _____

3. You can eat an apple. _____

4. All grass is purple. _____

5. A chair can lay an egg. _____

6. You can hear with your ears. _____

7. A goat has four legs. _____

8. You can see with your nose. _____

79

True or False Time

Write a T beside the sentence if it is true and an F if the sentence is false.

1. You go fishing in a lake. _____

2. A farmer has wings. _____

3. You can smell with your hands._____

4. A pilot flies a plane. _____

5. A snake has legs. _____

6. A fish can walk fast. _____

7. A dog can drive a car. _____

8. A bird can fly. _____

9. A whale is a big animal. _____

10. A giant is very little. _____

11. A boy has eleven fingers. _____

12. The sun is very hot. _____

80

How Do They Feel?

Underline the sentence that tells how the person in the story feels.

Little Red Hen was eating corn in the barn-yard. She looked up and saw the fox coming right at her!

Little Red Hen was happy.

Little Red Hen was hungry.

Little Red Hen was afraid.

Uncle Carlos had a surprise for Rosa. She was going for her very first ride in an airplane!

Rosa was sad.

Rosa was happy.

Rosa was tired.

Sam had a new, toy truck. He took it to school to show his friends, but on the way home he lost it.

Sam was happy.

Sam was sad.

Sam was funny.

81

How Do They Feel?

Underline the sentence that tells how the person in the story feels. ☺ ☹

"Look at it rain," said Bill. "Now I cannot fly my kite."

    Bill was happy

    Bill was sad.

    Bill was funny.

"Oh, good!" said Maria. "It is my birthday. All of my friends are coming to my party."

    Maria was sad.

    Maria was happy.

    Maria was tired.

Ray and Tom were playing with Tom's new ball. Some big boys came and tried to take the ball. Ray and Tom ran away.

    Ray and Tom were happy.

    Ray and Tom were funny.

    Ray and Tom were afraid.

The Homework Booklet

What's It About?

Circle the picture that tells the main idea of the story.

A bird is an animal with feathers. Birds hatch from eggs. They have two legs and a beak. All birds have wings, but some birds cannot fly. Some children are called "bird-watchers" because they like to watch birds.

wing

children

bird

You can have a garden. First, plant some seeds, then water them. They will need warm sun, and then they'll begin to grow. Be sure to keep your garden free from weeds.

sun

garden

seeds

What's It About?

(Circle) the picture that tells the main idea of the story.

Rose has a new kite. It is blue and has a picture of the sun on it. It can fly very high but it cannot go up to the clouds.

sun

kite

clouds

A barn is a good home for animals. Cows, pigs, and horses live in a barn. A barn keeps the rain out, and it is a place for the animals to get food.

cow

rain

barn

84

Give Me a Title!

Underline the best title for each story.

You can make a boat from a bar of soap. The soap has a flat bottom. A stick and a piece of paper make the sail. You can play with your boat in the pond or in the tub.

Going to the Pond

A Soap Boat

Fun With a Car

Kim was a little lost kitten. She was lost in the tall grass. It was dark in the tall grass and Kim wanted something to eat. She wanted her mama. At last Kim saw something in the grass. It was mama! How happy Kim was.

The Little Lost Kitten

In The Grass

A New Mama

85

Give Me a Title!

Underline the best title for each story.

Mark and Jack wanted to do something new. They did not want to play ball. They did not want to play with their dog. "I know!" said Jack. "We can make a tree house." "That will be fun," said Mark. So the boys made a tree house.

The Ball Game

Fun With A Dog

The New Tree House

Great job! You're finished

You have finished this Book

There is a big park in the city. Many boys and girls come to the park to play. At the park they can play ball or ride their bikes. Some children bring their lunches and have a picnic.

The Bike Ride

Fun at the Park

The Ball Game

86